The Library of the Thirteen Colonies and the Lost Colony™

The Colony of New York

Susan Whitehurst

The Rosen Publishing Group's
PowerKids Press™
New York

For Jeannie

Published in 2000 by The Rosen Publishing Group, Inc.
29 East 21st Street, New York, NY 10010

Photo Credits: Book cover and title page, pp. 1, 12, 16 © Super Stock; pp. 2, 7, 8, 11, 12, 18, 19, 20, 22 © Granger Collection; p. 22 © FPG International; pp. 16, 20, 22 © Archive Photos.

First Edition

Book Design: Andrea Levy

Whitehurst, Susan.
     The Colony of New York / by Susan Whitehurst.
         p.   cm. — (The library of the thirteen colonies and the Lost Colony)
     Includes index.
     Summary: Relates the history of the colony of New York from its founding by the Dutch in 1609 to statehood in 1788.
     ISBN 0-8239-5478-1 (lib. bdg.)
     1. New York (State)—History—Colonial period, ca. 1600-1775 Juvenile literature. 2. New York (State)—History—1775-1865 Juvenile literature. [1.
     New York (State)—History—Colonial period, ca. 1600–1775. 2. New York (State)—History—1775-1865.]   I. Title. II. Series.
     F122 .W48 1999
     974.7'02—dc21   99-14961
                                                                                                                     CIP

Manufactured in the United States of America

Contents

New Netherland

The first people to live in the area that would later become New York were the Algonquian and Iroquois Indians. After Columbus brought news of America to Europe, people from European countries came there to live in **colonies**. The first Europeans to settle this area were Dutch people from a country called the Netherlands. In 1609, a Dutch explorer named Henry Hudson came to the northeastern coast of America. Hudson, who worked for a Dutch trading company, wasn't looking for a place to start a colony. He was looking for a river route that would take him to Asia. Instead, he found an area he called New Netherland.

◀ *This picture shows Henry Hudson's arrival on the coast of America.*

The First Settlement

In 1624, a company called the Dutch West India Company sent eighteen families to New Netherland. They built Fort Orange, where the city of Albany is today. The next year, more Dutch settlers began to build a town on Manhattan Island. They called it New Amsterdam, after a city in the Netherlands. In 1626, the colony's first **governor**, Peter Minuit, bought Man-a-hat-ta (Island of the Hills) from the Indians in exchange for knives, beads, and cloth worth about $24 altogether.

The colonists brought cows and horses with them. They built farms, houses, shops, and churches. The Dutch welcomed people from different countries and different religions. By 1640, people from England, Norway, Denmark, Germany, and Scotland all lived in New Netherland.

Peter Minuit bought Manhattan from the Indians. ▶

New Amsterdam

In 1647, the Dutch sent Peter Stuyvesant to be the second governor of New Netherland. Stuyvesant was nicknamed "Peg Leg Pete" because he had one wooden leg. He made the city of New Amsterdam cleaner and safer. He told colonists to lead their horses through the streets, instead of letting them run free. This kept the streets orderly. He formed the first kind of police department, called a "rattle watch." When a watchman saw trouble, he would shake a large rattle to call for help. Stuyvesant also hired men to collect garbage and had the city's first post office and hospital built.

Stuyvesant allowed horses and carts to be ridden on the colony's widest street—Broadway. Broadway is still a street in today's New York.

◀ *Peter Stuyvesant did a lot to help New Amsterdam, shown here in a painting.*

Fighting Over Land

By 1664, nine thousand people lived in New Netherland. The city of New Amsterdam was doing very well, too. Business was good, and there were shops, taverns, and bakeries. Not everything in New Netherland was going well, though. In the 1640s, Swedish settlers started a colony on Dutch land near New Amsterdam. In 1655, Governor Stuyvesant raised an army of men and took over the Swedish colony. Stuyvesant also led several wars against nearby Algonquian Indian tribes. These wars hurt both the Dutch and the Algonquians. Many colonists' homes, barns, and fields were destroyed. The Indians had to give up the land that they had lived on for hundreds of years.

Stuyvesant and the Dutch speak peacefully with local Indians here, but sometimes there was trouble. ▶

The English Take Over

In 1664, King Charles II of England sent his brother James, the Duke of York, to take New Netherland from Stuyvesant and the Dutch. New Netherland was renamed New York after James. At first, James let the colonists vote to choose their laws and leaders. Then, in 1686, these rights were taken away. James said that New York was no longer its own colony, but was a part of a larger colony called the Dominion of New England. James put an English governor named Sir Edmund Andros in charge of the Dominion. Andros said that the colonists couldn't vote for their leaders. He also said that all the colonists' land belonged to England. The people of the Dominion were so angry that a mob chased Andros from the colony.

◀ *This portrait of James, Duke of York, is shown against a picture of Stuyvesant giving New Netherland to the English.*

Rich and Poor

In 1691, New York became a royal colony and was ruled by the king and queen of England. New York did not grow as quickly as some of the other colonies. Many colonists didn't want to live there. When the Dutch first settled the area, they gave large areas of land to a few very wealthy men. These men were called **patroons**. Other colonists had to pay rent to live and farm on the patroons' land. When the English took over New York, this system continued. The **tenant farmers** who worked the land felt that rents were too high. Sometimes tenant farmers rebelled against the landowners.

A wall was built to protect the north end of early New York City. The wall was torn down. Wall Street, a business area, is there today.

Tenant farmers got angry because they had to work for the patroons before they could work on land for themselves.

At War With the French

In the late 1600s, and throughout the 1700s, New York continued to have problems. Both England and France had colonies in North America, and wanted to control the land. In 1689, the French and their Indian **allies** started a war when they attacked an English town. War began again in New York in 1702, and once again in 1744. Many people were killed, and homes and farms were destroyed. New colonists were afraid to come to New York. In 1754, the last war between the French and the English began. This war, called the French and Indian War, would last until 1763. In the end, the English won, and the French were forced to give up their land in North America.

◀ *After the French and Indian War, the English were in control of much of North America.*

French & Indian War ▶

The Stamp Act Congress

The wars with France cost England a lot of money for soldiers, weapons, and forts. To pay off their war **debts**, the English decided to **tax** the colonists for sugar and paper. The tax on paper was called the Stamp Act, because a stamp had to be put on all paper to show that the tax had been paid. The colonists were angry about the taxes. They didn't think it was fair to have to pay taxes that they hadn't voted for. In October 1765, men from nine colonies met in New York City at a meeting called the Stamp Act Congress. The colonists decided they wouldn't buy any goods that came from England. Afraid of losing money, the king gave in. In 1766, he canceled the Stamp Act. New York's Stamp Act Congress had won.

Angry colonists protested against the tax on stamps by burning paper. ▶

At War With England

The king of England started taxing the colonists for other goods besides paper. Then he sent soldiers to the colonies. In April 1775, fighting broke out between British soldiers and the American **militia**. The **Revolutionary War** had begun. In New York City, colonists chased the English governor out of town. They tore down a statue of King George III and melted it to make 42,000 bullets. In August 1776, English ships and soldiers captured the city. After eight years of fighting, the colonies would win and become the United States of America.

During the Revolutionary War, 10,000 Americans died in New York Harbor. They died of hunger or disease on British prison ships.

◀ *Colonists tore down a statue of King George III in New York City. After the war, George Washington and his troops proudly entered New York to take it back from the British.*

The Empire State

On July 26, 1788, New York voted to accept the Constitution. New York City was the new nation's first capital. George Washington was sworn in as the first president in 1789 at Federal Hall on Wall Street. He called New York the "Empire State," because he believed that New York would be the center of the American **empire**. The state that began with eighteen Dutch families is now home to millions.

1609
Henry Hudson claims land for the Dutch.

Peter Minuit buys Manhattan from the Indians.

1626

1664
England takes over New Netherland, and it becomes New York.

The French and Indian War begins.

1754

1775
The Revolutionary War begins.

New York becomes a state.

1788

Glossary

allies (A-lyz) Groups of people that agree to help another group of people.

colonies (KAH-luh-neez) Areas in a new country where a large group of people move who are still ruled by the leaders and laws of their old country.

debts (DEHTS) Money that someone has borrowed and has not yet paid back.

empire (EM-pyr) A large area under one ruler.

governor (GUH-vuh-nur) An official that is put in charge of a colony by a king or queen.

militia (muh-LIH-shuh) A group of people who are trained and ready to fight, but who are not the army.

patroons (puh-TROONZ) The owners of large areas of land in Colonial New York.

Revolutionary War (REH-vuh-LOO-shuh-nayr-ee WOR) The war that American colonists fought from 1775 to 1783 to win independence from England.

tax (TAKS) When the government makes people give money to help pay for public services.

tenant farmers (TEH-nint FAR-murz) Farmers who pay rent to work on someone else's land.

Index

Web Sites:

You can learn more about Colonial New York on the Internet. Check out this Web site:
http://www.ci.nyc.ny.us/nyclink/html/misc/html/1998/colonialny.html